I0480385

MINIMALIST BUDGET

Simple Strategies On How To Save More and Become Financially Secure.

CHARLIE MASON

TABLE OF CONTENTS

Introduction

This book contains proven steps and strategies on how to save more and become financially secure. Are you one of those people who cannot leave a shopping mall or an online retail store without purchasing anything? Do you find yourself out of money long before your next paycheck? Does your budget seem so stretched out yet you still seem to lack so many things? If you answered yes to all these questions and are looking for ways to make your paycheck last longer, the solution is to adopt the concept of a minimalist budget. This concept will help you understand the reasons why you spend, provide you with ideas on how curb your impulse buying tendencies and save you money. It will show you how much better your life can become even without spending a lot of money. You will also get tips on how to save more and improve your spending habits. This book will help you become more in control of your money and your finances and show you the many money saving tips that will help you save more and spend less. If you're ready to start saving, turn to the next page and see what's in store for you.

CHAPTER 1

The Psychology of Purchasing

There are many reasons why people buy things, but psychology will tell you that there are 4 most basic psychological behaviors that help you understand why you buy what you buy. These four factors according to psychologists also predict the things that you will buy in the future.

Factor #1 – Satisfaction of Needs

This is the most basic reason why people purchase stuff - because of a need that they have to fulfill. Most of the things that people buy are bought because there is some intrinsic need that they have to fulfill. Needs can be classified as basic or complex.

Basic needs are those that fulfill your base requirements. These base requirements are often associated to physical needs. Things that your body needs to function normally are called basic needs. Examples of basic needs are food, water, and shelter.

Complex needs are those that fulfill your emotional, spiritual, and other forms of non-physical need. These can include having friends, belonging to a group, or taking on a hobby that relaxes you. Complex needs sometimes overlap with the other need psychological reasons why people buy things.

Factor #2 – Attention and Perception

This psychological factor in purchasing is the thing that advertisers and marketing teams have influence over. These two go hand in hand because perception is often dependent on attention.

An advertiser's goal is to get the attention of the customers long enough for them to build a perception on the product that they are selling. Perception can be favorable or not. The goal is always to create a favorable one so people will want to buy the product.

 To capture the buyer's attention, advertisers make sure that their advertisement is catchy, witty, and truly attention grabbing. Some advertisers use special effects, unusual ideas, and gimmicks just to get the buyer to look at their product or make the buyer aware that such a product exists.

Once the buyer's attention is caught, he can form a perception on the type of product being sold. If he finds that the product makes him feel good or fulfills his needs, the buyer will more often than not, buy that item. If he does not feel that the item is not going to be of any use to him or if he dislikes the message that the advertisement is sending, the buyer will not likely want to buy that product.

Most advertisers know that perception can be altered. That is why they use a tactic called repetition and distortion.

Repetition is when they keep showing the product in different channels where a buyer will be most likely to see it. These channels include TV, print, and online. The more a person sees these repetitive advertisements, the more the products stick to their minds. This makes it easier for them to recall the marketing message when they are faced with this product in a supermarket for example. The familiarity makes a person more enticed to buy it.

Distortion is a form of manipulation of the person's perception to make the product more favorable in the eyes of the buyer. A good example of distortion is making something that is often perceived as a bad thing look good. A gun, for example, is something that people would associate with death or as weapons that can harm people. But gun manufacturers would market it as a form of protection or something that can keep the persons you love safe.

Factor #3 – Knowledge and Conditioning

To buy a product, most people will do their research about that particular product. This is true for items that the person has never used before or items that are expensive. An average person will find out everything he can about the product before making that purchase.

Some people are influenced by knowledge about the product as provided by other people. If the knowledge about the product is not good, an advertiser's job is to condition the person to change his perception by presenting him with a different set of knowledge that will appeal to him before he can be convinced to buy the product.

Knowledge and learnings from other people's experience also influence the way people buy things. This is the reason why people turn to reviews, unboxing, samples, and try-before-you-buy promos before they buy into what the advertisers are saying. Reviews show the buyer an actual encounter with the product without buying the product.

Factor #4 – Beliefs, Cultures, and Attitudes

A big factor in the psychology of purchasing is a person's set of beliefs, cultures, and attitudes. A person can be influenced into buying something because it is something that has been inculcated in his system even before he has formed his perception about a particular product. It is something that has become a habit and permanent thing in a person's life.

A good example of this is when a person does not buy pork because his belief dictates that pork is an animal that is associated with a scavenger that eats dirt and muck. People with this belief are taught early on in their life that pork is dirty so they avoid it at all costs.

These are just some of the most common psychological factors that can explain why people buy or don't buy a particular item. There are more reasons that are often far more complex than these four. These complex reasons are often combinations of these four basic influencers.

CHAPTER 2

How to Ignore Advertisements

Advertisements are created mainly to give customers an idea of what products are available in the market and to entice them to buy these products. They would be shown on TV, print, and on the internet. Big companies pay top dollar to get the best time slot on TV or the billboard spot along the busiest roads. They also pour huge amounts of money on marketing teams and creatives in order to get ahead of the competition.

Unless you live under a rock, you cannot truly escape advertising. It comes from so many different channels that it's hard to really block them off completely. But there is a way to ignore them. Some of the most effective ways are detailed here:

1. Lessen Your Exposure – TV and the internet are some of the most common places where advertising thrives. Lessen your exposure to these channels and you lessen your exposure to advertisements. When watching TV, for example, you can try standing up and doing other things during commercial breaks instead of sitting through the ads and mindlessly watching them. Watching commercials make the products repetitive and easy to recall to make you more susceptible to impulse buys.

2. You can use commercial breaks to go to the bathroom, do some sit ups, talk with the person you are sitting beside, or check your email. Put the TV on mute while the commercials are on to ensure that you don't hear anything.

3. Adblocking Software – if you must use the internet (as almost everyone does), you can find a good adblocking software that can filter advertisements so you don't have to see them or see them as often. These adblockers often come with a price. Choose one that will fit your needs and your budget.

4. Use Subscription Services – Some subscription services such as Netflix allow you to watch TV without commercials interrupting you every 10 seconds. You will need to pay for these services on a monthly basis but you can be assured that you need not see an ad while you are enjoying your show.

5. Increase your Knowledge – the more you know about a product, the less likely you are to acknowledge the promos and gimmicks that other advertisements are parading. You can ignore an advertisement better if you know a product inside and out. Knowing the ins and outs of your favorite products make you less susceptible to buying a new product just because it has the words NEW and IMPROVED stamped in front of its packaging.

6. Avoid Window Shopping – for some, this may be hard to do. But avoiding the shopping mall or the online shop altogether is one of the best ways to ignore advertisements. Instead of window shopping, use your time for more productive yet equally enjoyable activities. Write on your journal, go for a jog, read a book, or take up a new hobby.

7. Learn to be Content with What You Have - One of the reasons why advertisements work is that they would always try to convince the customers that they need that particular product in their life in order to live better. But when a person is content with what he has,

he becomes less inclined to buy that product. If your phone is still working and serving its purpose, for example, and you are content with its performance, you will not think about replacing it as soon as the new model comes out. You will not want the new features as much because you are satisfied with your phone.

8. Be Alert – be wary of advertisements that offer miracle cures and unbelievable claims. These advertisements are often presented in the form of infomercials. Although their claims border on the impossible, all the information, research findings, expert opinion, and testimonials that they put in their infomercials convince consumers of their product's effectiveness. Be wary of these tactics and do not immediately fall for these false advertisements.

9. Get Rid of Temptation – Don't take flyers handed out at the malls, get rid of spam and junk mail, and do not subscribe to retail newsletter or text alerts. These tell you more about new products that you can spend on. The less you know, the better you will be at not buying anything. Besides, if you really need something, you will definitely go out and search for it. You do not have to yield to the marketers when they tell you that you need their products.

You may find it hard to do these things at first especially if your habits include the activities you need to avoid i.e. watching TV mindlessly. But with practice and a good amount of willpower, you can become an expert at ignoring advertisements. Keep practicing and soon it will become second nature to you that you don't notice yourself doing it anymore.

CHAPTER 3

How to Get Over Compulsive Spending Habits

Compulsive spending as defined by many psychological experts is a human behavior wherein a person would put a huge amount of time and effort in buying things to a point that it strains or impairs his life and relationships.

This manner of spending is considered a psychological problem that often requires intervention and help from qualified therapists. It is sometimes considered as a form of addiction because a person experiences a natural high whenever he acquires an item. That high can be addicting to the point that a person loses money and property and severs relationships.

The most common effect of compulsive shopping for some people is the feeling of happiness. Compulsive spenders feel happy every time they purchase something. But they instantly regret it because it usually eventually leads to getting deep in debt. They tend to buy stuff whenever they are depressed or sad to make them happy. Their shopping habits get out of hand and sometimes lead to disagreements and discord between them and the people they love. Rifts start to form until families are torn apart all because of this addiction.

To help you get over your compulsive spending habits, here are some of the most effective ways.

Cut Up Your Credit Cards – some people don't see credit cards as harmful because they don't see actual money being exchanged between them and the retail shop. This gives you the illusion that you are not really spending any money. You become more confident at spending because you see that you still have a balance on your bank account. But when the bill comes, you will realize that you have more purchases than money in the bank.

The best way to ensure that you don't spend unnecessarily you should know where your money is going. It is best for you to spend using cash. When you see your money dwindling, you will be less likely to keep buying.

Bring Exact Amounts – you know how much the bus fares are. Your lunch money or food allowance for the day should also be budgeted so you know your limit. Bring only that much money for the day so you will not be tempted to buy something while you are cruising along the mall.

If you are afraid that you will be caught in an emergency, you can bring enough money to get you home, but make sure that it's not in the same pocket or wallet as your spending money so do not "accidentally" spend it. Use it for actual emergencies only.

Track the Things That You Buy – when you track the things that you purchase, you are less likely to buy duplicate things. It also helps you become more conscious of your spending. Tracking your spending will help you understand where your money is going. Make a list using an app or the note function of your phone to make it easy.

Wait Before Buying – Buy an item only after waiting for some time. Around 30 – 60 minutes is a good amount of time to wait. When you see an item that you really want to buy, your body becomes excited and logic often flies out the door. Calm yourself down and walk away from that item. If, after some time, you still cannot forget that item or feel that you still need it, that is the time to buy. Chances are, once you have walked away, your brain has seen the logic and you will realize that you don't need another pink shirt as you already have 10 at home.

Use a List and Stick to It – The supermarket is a prime trap for impulse buys. With so many items around competing for your attention, it's so hard not to give in and pluck them out from the shelves and put them on your cart. But if you have a list and know the exact places to find the items on your list, you are less likely to wander through aisle after aisle of food and grocery items.

Get the Help of a Buddy – Find people whose willpower is stronger than yours and bring them along with you on your shopping trips. They will help remind you of your no buying policy. Just make sure that you adhere to their reminders otherwise it is futile to bring them along if you are just going to ignore their advice.

Do Something Else Every Time You Feel Like Shopping – Go for a walk, exercise, continue your hobby, or sleep. Keep yourself busy so you don't think of shopping.

The key to getting over your compulsive spending is self-control and self-awareness. Once you have control over your urges and are able to channel them to better activities, you are less likely to give in to the call of retail therapy.

CHAPTER 4

Increase Your Self-Confidence
With Budgeting

Budgeting is an age old practice where people allocate funds for things that they need to purchase or save for. People who budget their money would plan out how the money gets spent so that all bills are taken care of and needs are met. It is here that you take into consideration your income and match it with the things that you need in order to live a comfortable life.

For some people, budgeting is hard especially when their means or sources of income are limited. But with minimalist budgeting, a budget is always possible no matter how small your income is.

What is a Minimalist Budget?

A minimalist, loosely defined, is someone who uses only a few items in his life and does not feel the need to fill it with material things. You'll see minimalists sometimes living with less than 100 items and still they feel happy despite not having what others consider as luxuries in life.

A minimalist budget is something similar. People who are experts at this kind of budget are mostly minimalists by nature. They keep things simple so they don't have to spend as much. They value quality over quantity so their material possessions last longer than most items in a regular person's closet. They are more discerning and are concerned more about durability and longevity rather than popularity and aesthetics.

Minimalist budgets do not always mean that you have to spend less. Most of the items that minimalists purchase are of high quality so it can sometimes be more expensive in the beginning but will also pay off in the end. Buying a high quality product means that they don't have to keep replacing the product over a long time since it is more durable and long wearing.

Improve Your Self-Confidence in Budgeting With These Tips

To truly create a minimalist budget and improve your self-confidence with budgeting, you can try these simple ideas. These will help you manage your spending without making you feel like you are losing out. These will also help you transition into a full pledged minimalist budget:

1. Find out where your money goes – the first thing you need to do is to list down your expenses. Listing down your expenses will help you identify your spending traps. Is it clothes? Is it too much expensive coffee from your local coffee shop? Once you find out where your money traps are, you will be able to consciously avoid them. If you must have a budget for these expenses, you can put a cap or a limit to the amount that you spend.

2. Allocate amounts to more important items first – list down the things that need to be paid and when they are due. Set aside the money for these expenses as soon as you get your income. Make sure that you don't touch that money for other things.

3. Some people use the envelope method where they put the money in different envelopes. When it's time to pay these expenses, they simply take out that particular envelope while the rest remains untouched.

4. Seek the help of everyone in your household – if you are

the only one doing the budgeting while the rest of your family are wastrels, you'll end up frustrated and resentful of everyone around you. Creating a minimalist budget entails the inputs and cooperation of the people around you. You should get them to understand the reason for your budgeting so they don't feel deprived.

5. Compare Brands and Offers – when buying big ticket items, don't just jump at the first opportunity or deal that comes your way. Find out the best deals available before taking the plunge. Check also the payment plan so you are not surprised by the amount that you need to shell out in order to pay the installment or balance.

6. In buying cars for example, you should find out how long the warranties are, what are the inclusions upon purchase and the other important details. Factor in the monthly payments to your budget and see if you need to make cuts to make it work. Don't just buy because the down payments are low. You could end up paying more in monthly installments.

7. Allot an amount for savings – having a nest egg that you never touch is something that can provide you with a feeling of security and safety. It is important to budget for savings so that come rainy day or when faced with tough situations that require cash, you are covered. The general rule is to allot 20% of your income to savings but you can add more if you are able.

8. Know what is available – some people go shopping to buy something only to find that they already have it at home. They end up having multiples of the same products. When you know what you have and don't have, you are not likely to go shopping just because you cannot find it.

9. Budget for incidentals – Emergencies or incidentals can include a car breaking down and sickness or disability. These instances are often not within your control but will affect your life in a big way. Include these items in you budget so your income or your savings will not take a big blow in case you encounter such instances.

Budgeting gets easier the more you practice it. Be in the habit of budgeting instead of going shopping without a plan. Budgets may feel constraining to some but when you get used to it, you will see that it is always more economical than buying mindlessly. With enough practice, you can become confident in your budgeting abilities and eventually curb your mindless spending tendencies.

CHAPTER 5

Improve Your Spending Habits

Now that you know how to budget, it's time to focus on your spending habits. Your spending habits are the things that define how you use your money. Bad spending habits are characterized by impulse buys, buyers regret and increased debt. Good spending habits, on the other hand, help you get out of debt, give you financial freedom and make you feel secure in your future.

To improve your spending habits, you need to know what is triggering them. For some people, they spend more when they feel sad or depressed. Other people feel like spending when they are happy. Again that mood factor comes to mind. This is not the right way to go.

Shopping when you are depressed, sad, or feeling emotional will make it easy for you to spend more. Your mind will reason out that you had a very bad day and that you need something new to keep you happy. This is only temporary happiness. You will feel a high on your purchase but will soon feel buyer's remorse especially when you realize that you cannot afford to pay for that item. You will also feel like you are drowning in debt which will continue the cycle of depression further.

When you are feeling sad, you should avoid going to shopping malls or to places where you will most likely spend money. Go for activities that will take your mind off your sadness. Things like playing with pets at the park, reading a good book, or writing on your journal will occupy you and take your mind off your sadness. These activities are also not that expensive. You can also try doing something productive. Channel your sadness to art and music and create songs or works of art. You'll be able to release your sadness and create something beautiful at the same time.

Another trigger to spending is happiness. Getting that bonus at work for a job well done can make you feel like a one-time millionaire. This usually makes you feel like indulging and spending tons of money to celebrate your success. While there is nothing wrong with celebrating achievements it is also important to note that too much spending will deplete your funds or bonus so you are back to living off paycheck to paycheck. Don't make this mistake and use up all your money in one go. Allocate them to the right channels i.e. savings, expenses, and other important things before using it up celebrating.

When you come across a windfall or cash inflow, the best thing to do to curb spending is to step back and just breathe. The natural high that you feel from receiving the money will wear off eventually and you will feel more in control of your spending habits. You will gain a more reasonable perspective once the initial thrill has gone and will be less likely to spend.

The best time to go shopping is when you are not feeling a lot of tumultuous and extreme emotions that can influence your spending habits. Shop only when you feel level-headed. Most people also suggest shopping after you have eaten because when you are hungry, you are more likely to spend on things to mask the feeling of hunger.

Another way to improve your spending habits is to become aware of yourself. You should know the underlying cause why you are spending more than necessary. When you know the reasons why, you are better able to avoid these causes so you will never feel the need to spend more.

CHAPTER 6

Savings Strategy to Get Out of Debt

Debt is something that everyone experiences at some point in life. If you are in a lot of debt because of your spending and you feel like you will never be free of debt, don't despair. There is still a way to get out of it. To help get out of debt, you need to have the right attitude in spending and saving.

When a person's attitude about spending is sound, he is able to control his spending better and walk away from the temptation of purchasing. People without the right attitude towards spending, like those who see spending as something they are entitled to, will find it so hard to stop himself from buying even if he does not have money anymore.

Saving is one of the best ways to get out of debt. But how do people use savings to do this? Aren't you supposed to pay off everything with the money that you have instead of putting it away as savings? Here's how it's done.

Savings, loosely defined, is an amount of money that you put away to use for the rainy days. When your savings is greater than your debt, you feel more secure about your future. To use savings to get out of debt, you will need to diligently put away the same amount or a greater amount of money regularly.

For example, if you are earning $1,000 a month and you have a debt of $60,000. From your monthly income, you allocate the monthly amount for your regular installments to pay off that debt. At the same time, set aside an amount of money to put away as savings. Once you have accumulated enough money as savings, say $10,000, you can put that savings to good use by paying off a big chunk of your debt. Paying off that much will lessen the interest rates because the principal amount has been decreased further.

While accumulating savings may not always be the easiest way to get out of debt especially if you have a lot of expenses, it is still one of the most effective ways. You should try saving any amount of money to later on use for making lump sum payments for your debt. Apply that lump sum to the principal amounts and soon your debts decrease substantially and you will be debt-free sooner than you expect.

CHAPTER 7

Money Management Guide

Managing your money is the process of tracking, budgeting, saving, and investing your money. It is the process that describes what you do with the money that you earn to make it grow and earn bigger yields. For some people, managing money comes very easily. These people usually have a very good knowledge about the financial world. For others, money management might just as well be a foreign language that needs to be deciphered using the Rosetta stone.

To manage money effectively, one of the things that you have to do is to embrace living frugally. To live frugally means that you do not live beyond your means. You only spend on necessities and do not indulge in luxuries too often. You don't waste money on non-essential needs. To do this, you need to distinguish which items are wants and which ones are needs. Spend money only on the things that you need and forget about the extras.

Another way for you to manage your money is by planning your expenses. Create a chart or a schedule that will tell you right away the expenses that you need to pay and when they are due. This ensures that you never miss a payment and incur late penalties in the process. An expense planner also allows you to see where your money really goes and which expenses are really eating up a huge chunk of your cash.

Expert money managers don't buy a 5 dollar coffee when he can brew his own coffee at home for less than a dollar per small cup. This is another way to manage your money. Be smart enough to know when where you can save. Money managers know how to identify the parts of their spending that they can do without and cut these effectively. This translates to bigger savings.

Manage your money with sound investments. This may seem easier said than done but it is one of the best and most effective ways to grow and manage your money. When you invest your money, you are not just letting it sit in the bank doing nothing. You are actually using your money to fund projects that will yield dividends and earnings for you. A successful venture will gain you added income in the form of interest rates on your funds.

CHAPTER 8

Feel Financially Secure Every Day

To feel financially secure every day means that you do not have to worry about your future finances. Not many people are able to say that they are financially secure because they don't feel like they have done enough to secure a comfortable future. But just because you don't feel financially secure now does not mean that you will never be. Here are some ways to lessen your financial security worries today and in the future:

1. Build up a solid savings account – knowing that you have something tucked away to use in case of emergencies provides you with a feeling of financial security like no other. With a big savings account, you won't feel like you will end up penniless when you grow old and become unable to work for a living.

2. Buy insurance – an insurance policy is another safety net that helps protect you in case of huge money losses. Some insurance policies that you can buy include life policy, disability policy, and retirement.

3. Invest wisely – people who are financially secure don't just feel happy having a huge savings account. They feel more secure when they know that they have invested their money in places that yield bigger rewards. They invest in things that are proven to be money makers.

4. Declutter and live minimally – people with so many things worry about the upkeep and maintenance of their material possessions. These hinder them from feeling like they are in control of their spending. To make sure that you don't spend too much, you should

let go of non-essential items and live with just the necessary things. When you have less material possessions to worry about, you will feel more secure about your future.

5. Save no matter how little amount you can – putting something in your savings account, no matter how small that amount is will still contribute to your financial security. Make it a habit to put in something in your savings.

Conclusion:

I hope this book was able to help you to understand the reasons why you spend, provide you with ideas on how curb your impulse buying tendencies and save you money. Remember, there are steps that you can do today in order to ensure that you will not have to worry about whether or not you will have enough money during your sunset years. It only takes some discipline in saving more and a whole lot of restraint when it comes to spending. Finally, if you found this book useful in any way, a review on Amazon is always appreciated!

www.ingramcontent.com/pod-product-compliance
Lightning Source LLC
Chambersburg PA
CBHW072034230526

45468CB00021B/1801